Jamaican Landscape

JAMAICAN LANDSCAPE

a volume of poems

R. GERALLT JONES

CHRISTOPHER DAVIES (PUBLISHERS) LTD.
LLANDYBIE, CARMARTHENSHIRE

First Published in mcmlxix
by Christopher Davies (Publishers) Limited
Swansea and Llandybie
Printed in Wales
by Merlin Press
Llandybie
All rights reserved

Published by Christopher Davies
with the support of The Welsh Arts Council

*for all at M T C
and particularly for Ken Thaxter*

Contents

A Letter at Christmas	*page*	11
He and I		12
Chameleon Man		13
Though the Stars Stare so Clear		14
Cocktail Party		15
Night		16
Poinsiana		17
Flame of the Forest		18
Cockroach		19
North Coast		20
Pedro Plains		21
Montego Bay		22
A Gravestone in the Blue Mountains		23
Of a Boy and his Teacher		24
Jamaican Girl		25
And so the Man Lives		26
Elegy for a Country Girl		27
Donald Burns Sangster		28
This Girl		29
Under Green Trees		30
His Plot of Land		31
On seeing an Old Man in the rainy season		32
From this, my balcony		33
The Sting		34
On reading an essay on patriotism		35
On leaving Jamaica		36

Preface

These poems were written during a stay of two years in Jamaica between 1965 and 1967. They are written in English, rather than, as would be more natural, in Welsh, partly because the experiences they attempt to express were lived out in an English context, linguistically speaking, and partly because I wished it to be possible for some of my many friends in Jamaica to have the opportunity of reading them. They make no attempt to present an ordered or a consistent reaction to Jamaica but they do represent for me some of the shreds and patches of a most moving and rewarding experience. I offer them, for what they are worth, to all those who were in any way connected with Mandeville Teachers' College when I was there, for that college and the experiences we shared in establishing it will always remain the focus and heart of my own personal Jamaica.

1969   *R. Gerallt Jones.*

A Letter at Christmas

By fireside table,
snowbound here,
I cannot see green cane
or that brown beauty;
it lives too far.
Hot winter, young banana flower,
warmed stone in the sun
that stretches corn
and kneads, feeds into life
limbs smooth and charged,
eyes deep as Blue Hole's terror,
dark as grottoes,
beautiful as children Sunday-dressed;
I cannot feel that land,
only its cold absence
now by this fire,
while letters move,
scrawled words,
licked flap,
thumped stamp,
from snow to sun
and image wilts
and cramps in this dry cold.

He and I

I'm white
he's black,
all right, who cares?
We can survive our bloody history
only by sitting still
and bathing our red wounds
in this white light.
I now no slaveship captain,
he no slave,
we sit and watch the warm sea rolling in
yet are betrayed.
I see his jutting lips
and barbed-wire hair
and think of foul and festering caves
plunging fetid through clean waves
and know who held the whip.
He sees my pallid hands,
powerless now to hurt,
strumming his own dark tunes
on a bambolin he made;
he knows that I came free
across that bitter sea
to this green place.
Here, he and I, we sit,
heartbeats concurrent,
thought synchronised in our own time.
We rise and swim ashore to the hot sand
but God knows how or when
a man can snap
the chain his father forged.

Chameleon Man

Chameleon man, why not wear your black
with a flourish,
contrast like hell with the bark and leaf
of this pale coffee land,
forget the green tree-lizard's tricks
of multi-coat?

But you, like us,
coloured Welsh in this grey mould of Europe,
eaten through with rooting and uprooting,
you here manipulate
tongues which fail to speak
and creak and groan of captive
minds fighting free,
you change your colour too
as the bark and leaf change theirs,
and to be, like the lizard, adaptable,
is for you, like us,
a virtue,
chameleon man.

Though the stars stare so clear

The stars stare so clear
there's no cloud cover here for subtlety
and where the sun roars down
there's no shade for side-issues;
meaning must rocket direct,
poems erupt in the blood
where the warrior spathodea
thunders through throbbing earth
and nightfrog's insistence
needles the quiet trees.

Yet here too, conquering and alien,
words intervene;
verbiage, viscous,
learnt pat on the tongue,
colonises the heart
till light is lost in its foliage.

And so, sculpted in stubborn stone,
eyes emptied of sense,
an old negro stands on a stage,
seemly in steamed white collar
and three-buttoned suit
and speaks in abstract terms
of God and the moral law
to an audience of silent infants
and crumpled women in hats
though the stars stare so clear.

Cocktail Party

Oh the civilisation of sherry
before dinner at night.
The stillness of maids starched white,
the substance of chairmen chatting,
composure of minor officials,
the jolly evangelisation
of public relations men.

Oh the dignified calm of old houses,
their wooden floors shining clean
of the blood and sweat split over them;
old houses, watchmen of empire,
controlling their gentle integration,
their mildly multiracial parties
before dinner at night.

The story is told of a man of goodwill
who, salvaging a drowning hat,
never saw the man beneath;
and departed justifiably proud
to his fine house on the hill.

Night

Listen; it walks the earth.
Growth grips green path at night,
walks over footpath and field,
bahama grass and seagrape and sheamus,
corn choking the treetops,
undergrowth, overgrowth conquering all.

In bed in the belly of night, listen.
It walks the earth,
riding the cattle and frogs
from kneehigh sweet pasture
to the grass that's the cricket's forest,
and slinks slow to each bedside
as water flows in a dream
deliberate, cold and smooth . . . .

Poinsiana

It's so light the wonder is,
on a morning so gusty,
that it fails to fly,
quivering and sighing,
to the wind's bed.

No one could paint it,
unless his brush turned light-headed
from seeing it move,
and his fingers as halting as petals on grass.
Paint is no kin to the butterfly-dye that made it.

And of words, what can be said?
Only that,
crawling like worms on virgin page,
they bear as much likeness to this dancing glory
that hangs disembodied over dirty yards
as the tired trudge of an old poet
to the light-skirted, outreaching, lovely sway
of a girl in the morning who knows where she goes
and why she is going.

The Flame of the Forest

What is this sense-impression on the eye
that it should spur wild horses in the blood,
its tint and turn a lake in the mind's desert?

Green paint on green ground
as the flowing once of velvet on high thrones
or a wave, ocean born, poised on precipice,
or soft pad for red rockets
threatening heaven from their nests,
or perhaps just a heavy tree whose generous flowers
dignify wood in a green land.

Infinite unity
with nowhere a line breaking
but where the sky's black
stops against the roof,
it surges through complaisant earth
as an old lion rises
to walk in his own wood,
vast so that size has no meaning,
strong until strength is cheap,
and at last nothing remains on the mind
but—for the lion—
dignity,
and for this tree colour through colour
flowing down sluggish artery,
the selfhood of its being straightening the mind,
firing peace in the marrow-bone.

Cockroach

Even its crunched death
is no matter for pity.
Patient and graceless,
bent on survival,
it carries its heavy blight,
feeling in corners,
infiltrating the dark,
and cannot be other than evil,
which also breeds in men's cuboards,
antennae sensitive as poets,
and scrabbles to hide in the heart's cracks,
swelling by night unnoticed,
and only dies desperate underfoot
when the violent light
blinds its deliberate march.

North Coast

On sale to the sun
like any unsatisfied whore
open to every brief spasm,
or like some baby teetering on sleep's edge
untroubled by light or dark.
Did smooth hip-swinging spring-heeled men
ever   hurry at leisure
on the ovenplates of its road,
or was the place
from the first lightburst of grace
as inorganic as this Sunday noon
and none but the sandflies busy?

Pedro Plain

Here on this Pedro Plain
what grows?
Man, that the sun
that up on Spur Tree heights
and by green Balaclava
nurtures flower and warms the running river
cracks dead earth here.

But these grim cattle live,
emaciated paps,
brittle bone,
moving like ghosts against the cactus thorn,
ochre-colour,
colour of parched soil,
they wander bodiless
or almost so,
nuzzling fibrous sisal,
passive in this sun,
and God, what grows
when milk is curdled in the udder
and hungry calves
shifting pathetic hooves on hot hard sand
gaze at this bitter land?

Montego Bay

The inappropriate
cocktail party shriek
of long Bermuda shorts
pervades the town.
Shaded in tall glass temples
pilfered from Miami Beach
where no viruses or babies breed
these mottled insects move,
putty-thighed, crook-backed, creak-kneed,
obscene in grey display
of shin and flank.

But down on Station Lane
where rotting timber harbours roach and pox
and glass unknown,
their lackeys move in beauty,
limber-limbed as lions,
trilby-hatted walk like gods
among those bitter shacks
and blackened corn
and love and loll
and viruses and babies are born.

A Gravestone in the Blue Mountains

Beyond all hope of hailing these ten years,
Adam Calvin Smith,
April, nineteen fifty seven,
a man, no doubt, of this mountain;
but here and now,
haphazard at nightfall
sense returns,
impulse and glimpse across these plunging heights,
uncertain,
ragged at first, but soon
great shadows gather round,
participants in an old pageant,
king and clown and king's impassive lords.

Fulsome, black-eyed girls,
flowing men, big-boned, easy and free,
calm in the grip of fate,
pilgrims commuting between blood and air,
spirits empty of motive:
all that multitude
of tongue-loose twisted poor
moved at the end into the dark
with one stark question
in the heart
but never asked
this side this stone.

Of a Boy and his Teacher

This is the dark in your bright land,
that so much love lies low,
sick, scared and wounded from the start,
strap-leathered underground.

How many faces, hostage-held
like his, gap-toothed,
flash trust this day
in squalid schools
at loveless, spattered walls
and narrow women long shut out
from that wide world of light?

Cracks open for him now
on desperate dreams,
sap stings old stems long dry
in all this knotted bitter room
where autumn rain spits at his grin
and grey wool-headed men
recall what once they were
and do not weep.

So may you, teacher, teach
among these desks scarred as sin
and playground bauxite-red,
so that one spark may not damp down
or so that newborn glimmers here and then,
caught in his offered eye,
may not all lie
dead in this windblown dust.

Jamaican Girl

You walk from womb to waste
in this hard land
where to be born woman
is to start wrong;
belted into beauty in the only way that was known,
leaving girlhood a scarred myth
where shinning trees was a morning's venture
into boyhood's strength and privilege.

But for all that whipping and moulding
here in the grim sun
you tread a sweet earth
that pours life into orange spathodea
and feeds the mischief of pink poinsiana
and thrusts impatient green through the red soil.

This they never beat from you
and may you walk to heaven in your land,
built around with quick movement,
hoarding behind still eyes
all that you saved of yourself,
banked fire and glow, slow hands
and a girl's knowing and challenge.
So deep from those swift limbs
may the dark sap of a fatherless nation
break out now into strong shoot
and blossom in loving and doing.

And so the Man Lives

(on the occasion of a folk concert in an Anglican church.)

And so again, this flyblown night,
he lives.
Forty kids whistle and blend in a marbled memorial
to the old colonial ways
on the ragged edge of the world;
an old creole in baggy suit
stares doe-eyed into space
and his fat brown wife remembers in disbelief
how she once played a pageant
and was Mary;
big, gentle faces peer in out of the night.

Inside, programmes flutter like neurotic leaves,
hot air wells up around the pews
in a tidal wave of sweat,
electric guitar chases mad, inexpressible griefs;
they sing of death and sink to surrender,
they sing of light and lapse into wordless sound;
girls' round voices mouth inexpressible joys,
and so again the man lives.

Here, lapped by the long-forgetting sea
in a still-forgotten country,
faces and hands can move,
fresh and unconquered by the slow paralysis of this land,
and incredibly,
as a boat slides without motion to a far jetty,
or as winter thaws unseen into crocus,
sense is touched,
silence is real,
deep images slip uneasy into sleeping minds
as a diver hits the air on burstling lungs.

Forty kids whistle and blend in this hot church,
and so again he lives.

Elegy for a Country Girl

A white owl hoots
somewhere beyond that royal palm,
buzzard squats ready, whistle
of frog from leaf-drowned town
clings on to day;
sunset unsettles shuttered windows,
cat stretches,
kerosene stove lies dead
inside the house; on rooftops
slates the rain
and rain-drops coldly greet the news.

Snatched from her dancing hill,
breadfruit blessed, to face
who knows what grim tribunal,
God grant she may have trial
in no seemly hymning place
but where crisp crust of Portland grass
cushions her feet,
sisal thrusts, goat bleats on hill's crown,
corntips climb the wind's cool,
the lighted town dull and far
and the night clear and glass.

She went from goat's path, windpath,
but rock stays green
and orchid white.
Night gathers gloomy on the peak
and now her dust in moving air
feeds rain and bitter storm.
What fisher's net
or pit or singing room
has swallowed her brown tumult in its peace?

Donald Burns Sangster *

They brought him home,
tidied him up
and showed him to the people.
As a symbol he was no great catch,
an ordinary man
coping, as ordinary men do,
or seeming to cope
until the end came.
But it served a purpose
and people wept
and flowers withered
swiftly in the sun.
Soldiers marched,
marble was quickly imported,
and then the litter remained,
coke bottles, crush barriers overthrown;
new rulers rode new cars
to their glass houses on hills
and life, except his, moved on.

*Prime Minister of Jamaica for four months in 1967, after being
deputy leader of his party for many years. He died
suddenly of coronary thrombosis, in Canada
and was later flown home.

This Girl

There, coloured by breadfruit dangling down
she sat, this girl,
and around her,
sad and pot-bellied
open-eyed with infancy and night,
six in facsimile,
tore at the mango flesh
with bitter teeth.

Over in the next tree's shade
a man stands
weight one-legged like a dark swan
making light of his masculinity
and watches as she sits,
watches her breath ease out
and shoulders shift
and hands move over thighs.

And so the darkness plummets down
rapid and clean tonight
blanketting them and all our doubts
and courting love and laughter
and after, sleep.

Under Green Trees

Under green trees,
feet flung out,
the freckle-haired quarter-back,
clean-vetted American boy
observes his hemisphere.
A Roman, you might say,
Civus Cincinnatti est,
however far from home.

Around and beyond
sing the green mountains,
beneath, wood-shackled fishnet beach,
hard black bodies cleave
spearing the syrup sea,
but here and now,
dateline Jamaica,
he writes airletters home
and sips his coke in a foreign land,
a modest conqueror
under green trees at night.

His plot of land

He decided one day
he'd dig this brown plot of land
in a welter of growth,
green growth and grasping.
And so he laboured
chopping in rhythm at roots and trees and stalks
hurling his wooden hoe through hard soil
muscles clenched under black skin
bared to the sun.
He planted corn in the rich dust
and pumpkin seed and yam
and built and roped, one day,
a cho-cho arbour for shade.
And so he dug
in this plot of land
and June came round
the corn stretched high
the sky climbed down to meet it
and the cho-cho roofed its arbour
and the yam grew ugly roots
and it all ended
where it all began.
His brown plot of land
in a welter of growth
grew prodigal green like the rest.

On seeing an old man in the rainy season

It's risky work old man
to walk the woods
this day, this rain
in case the tempted spirit gads
off, takes wing
leaves crumpled flesh
and heads for home
It's risky work old man to walk the woods.

Like one
when meeting slight acquaintance
for courtesy, that's all,
doffs his cap
keeps his distance
leaves intact the spirit's core
so this man meets the rain's disturbance
once, no more,
then turns for home
and leaves the rain to dance.

From this, my balcony

From this, my balcony,
     there's a black cloud gathering,
     been hovering long behind that roof.

Past this dark balcony
     through trellis of wet leaves
     I see the staring stars behind that roof.

On this warm balcony
     rocking my own way home
     I sleep sound in the sun that bakes that roof.

From this safe balcony
     crept on by orchids, shy at night,
     I loose the world and sail the changing sky
                         beyond that roof.

The Sting

Tears cannot hide
in this burnt light.

Not that the sting hurt
but that one gold and black aircraft
singing in air
declared war on your flesh.

World collapsed,
face fragmented,
as though creation had never been
nor the world set in order
and the face of an infant
had no limitation of bone.

Not that the sting hurt
for all this peevish finger-scratching
but the terror that a sunlit wonder
sailing the white sky
paused and left its arrow
in the apple of your mind's eye.

On reading an essay on patriotism

It's not that easy, man,
Jamaican or Welsh or what,
for patriots live by the bright sun's largesse,
feeding on day's elusive hopes
not the night's marauders,
the garish dreams that plunder sleep
dogging the day's brightness
down nightmare crooked ways.

Having walked, grey and introspective,
every forgotten path on these damned hills,
gazed, bewildered, down into valleys
no longer secret,
and hailed the unlistening sheep,
how can he prate of hope as sleep approaches?

He has not loved his blighted earth by choice
nor did he plead that life should breed his roots
on grass-forsaken hills;
but here he is, a seeker looking out
on bright horizons helplessly;
his dreamgirl never once inclines her eyes,
his dark coquette
simpers so many-sidedly
he cannot win.

On Leaving Jamaica

And so, unfussed, it flew,
the great white bird pouching its world inside it.
We are nowhere,
already futured,
when we flick back our seats
and curl in our packaged rest
(or if anywhere
inside ourselves
and as near limbo as anyone ever
this side of the dark.)

There's now nothing simple to say
but stare at the dim dark land
and forget;
existence being a quality in air,
a shifting anchor through time's shale,
and where there is no environment
there is no existence,
only the automatic reflex
and the yawn of body's slackness.

This perhaps
in coffined aluminium
is hell
if it goes on long enough.